STARGAZER

CALENDAR 2013

Monday	Tuesday	Wednesday	Thursday	Friday	Saturday	Sunday
31	01	02	03	04	05	06

JANUARY

**SILENCE TELEVISION
ILLUSTRATIONS & PRINTS**

Monday	Tuesday	Wednesday	Thursday	Friday	Saturday	Sunday
07	08	09	10	11	12	13

JANUARY

Kelli Anderson

Monday	Tuesday	Wednesday	Thursday	Friday	Saturday	Sunday
14	15	16	17	18	19	20

JANUARY

Astronaut Design

Navigation

Monday	Tuesday	Wednesday	Thursday	Friday	Saturday	Sunday
21	22	23	24	25	26	27

JANUARY

THE BEST THINGS in LIFE are MEANT to be SHARED

Lucille and William

B·R·O·O·K·L·Y·N

Dana Tanamachi

Monday	Tuesday	Wednesday	Thursday	Friday	Saturday	Sunday
28	29	30	31	01	02	03

FEBRUARY

Monday	Tuesday	Wednesday	Thursday	Friday	Saturday	Sunday
04	05	06	07	08	09	10

FEBRUARY

Brandan Deason

TOGETHER

Christ has designed us to live & work as a community dependent on each other.

Monday	Tuesday	Wednesday	Thursday	Friday	Saturday	Sunday
11	12	13	14	15	16	17

FEBRUARY

BACK FROM SPACE

Marius Roosendaal

Monday	Tuesday	Wednesday	Thursday	Friday	Saturday	Sunday
18	19	20	21	22	23	24

FEBRUARY

'82

Jonathan Mutch

Monday	Tuesday	Wednesday	Thursday	Friday	Saturday	Sunday
25	26	27	28	01	02	03

MARCH

Monday	Tuesday	Wednesday	Thursday	Friday	Saturday	Sunday
04	05	06	07	08	09	10

MARCH

Brandan Deason

Monday	Tuesday	Wednesday	Thursday	Friday	Saturday	Sunday
11	12	13	14	15	16	17

MARCH

Cristiana Couceiro

Monday	Tuesday	Wednesday	Thursday	Friday	Saturday	Sunday
18	19	20	21	22	23	24

MARCH

Darling Clementine

Monday	Tuesday	Wednesday	Thursday	Friday	Saturday	Sunday
25	26	27	28	29	30	31

MARCH

Mark Brooks

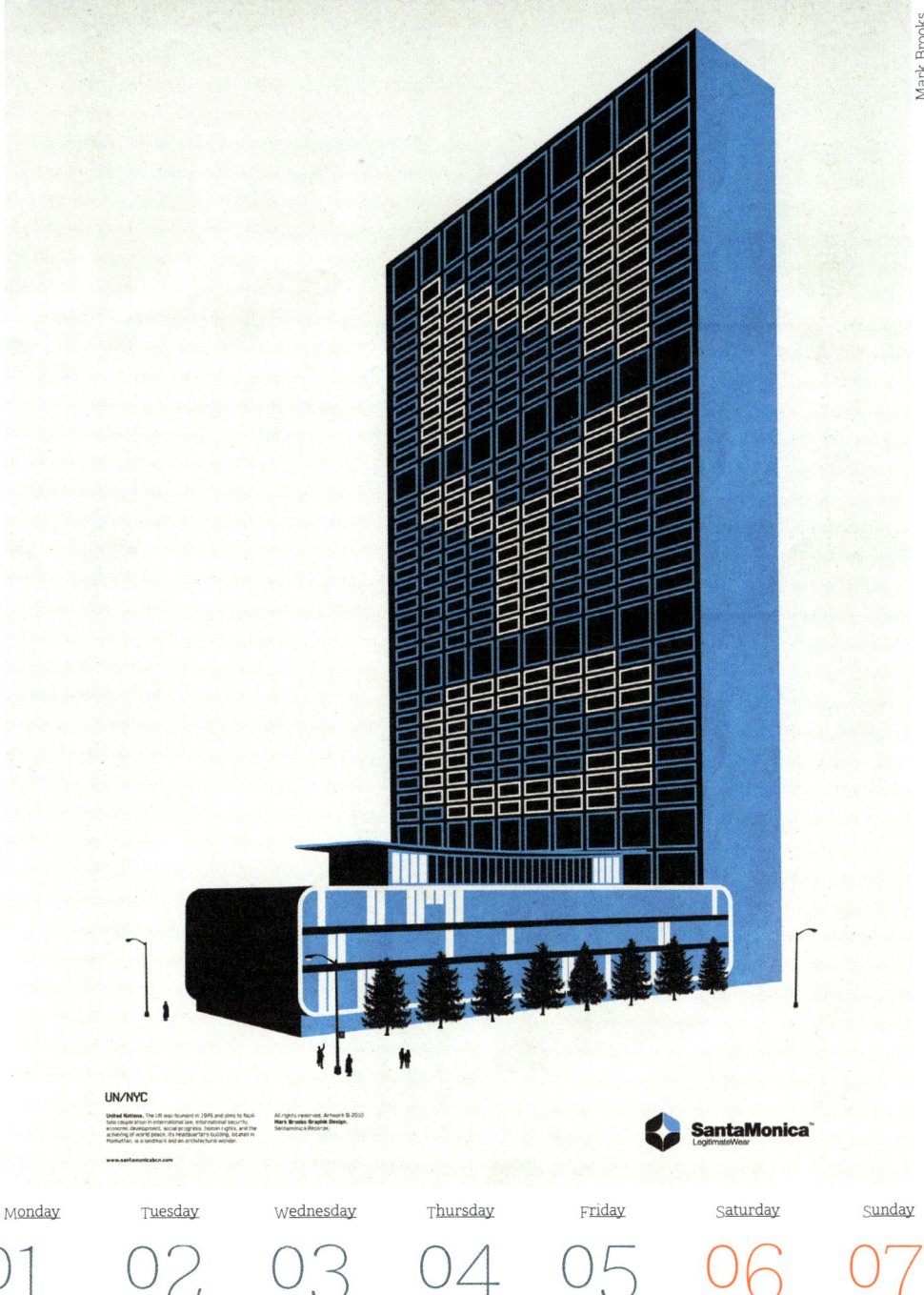

UN/NYC

United Nations. The UN was founded in 1945 and aims to facilitate cooperation in international law, international security, economic development, social progress, human rights, and the achieving of world peace. Its Headquarters building, located in Manhattan, is a landmark and an architectural wonder.

All rights reserved. Artwork © 2013
Mark Brooks Graphic Design.
Santamonica Rincon.

www.santamonicabcn.com

SantaMonica™
LegitimateWear

Monday	Tuesday	Wednesday	Thursday	Friday	Saturday	Sunday
01	02	03	04	05	06	07

APRIL

Andaur Studios

CAMERA

Monday	Tuesday	Wednesday	Thursday	Friday	Saturday	Sunday
08	09	10	11	12	13	14

APRIL

**FEBRUARY 17TH, 2010
DALLAS, TEXAS | HOUSE OF BLUES**

Jack's Mannequin

Sing for your Supper tour
WITH SPECIAL GUESTS FUN | VEDERA

Concepción Studios

WWW.CONCEPCIONSTUDIOS.COM

Monday	Tuesday	Wednesday	Thursday	Friday	Saturday	Sunday
15	16	17	18	19	20	21

APRIL

with SPECIAL GUESTS / NOVEMBER 3, 2009
THE EL MOCAMBO / TORONTO, ON

FUTURE OF THE LEFT

Doublenaut

Monday	Tuesday	Wednesday	Thursday	Friday	Saturday	Sunday
22	23	24	25	26	27	28

APRIL

Heath Killen

Monday	Tuesday	Wednesday	Thursday	Friday	Saturday	Sunday
29	30	01	02	03	04	05

MAY

Matt Lehman

Monday	Tuesday	Wednesday	Thursday	Friday	Saturday	Sunday
06	07	08	09	10	11	12

MAY

VELO

Doublenaut

Monday	Tuesday	Wednesday	Thursday	Friday	Saturday	Sunday
13	14	15	16	17	18	19

MAY

Riley Cran

SWALLOWED SUN
BREWING CO.
Seattle, Wa

Monday	Tuesday	Wednesday	Thursday	Friday	Saturday	Sunday
20	21	22	23	24	25	26

MAY

La Boca

Monday	Tuesday	Wednesday	Thursday	Friday	Saturday	Sunday
27	28	29	30	31	01	02

JUNE

MP567 $1.50

FAIRFAX/MOSGROVE PAPERBACKS

Julian Montague

Spider and I
Fausto Castillo

Monday	Tuesday	Wednesday	Thursday	Friday	Saturday	Sunday
03	04	05	06	07	08	09

JUNE

Matt Lehman

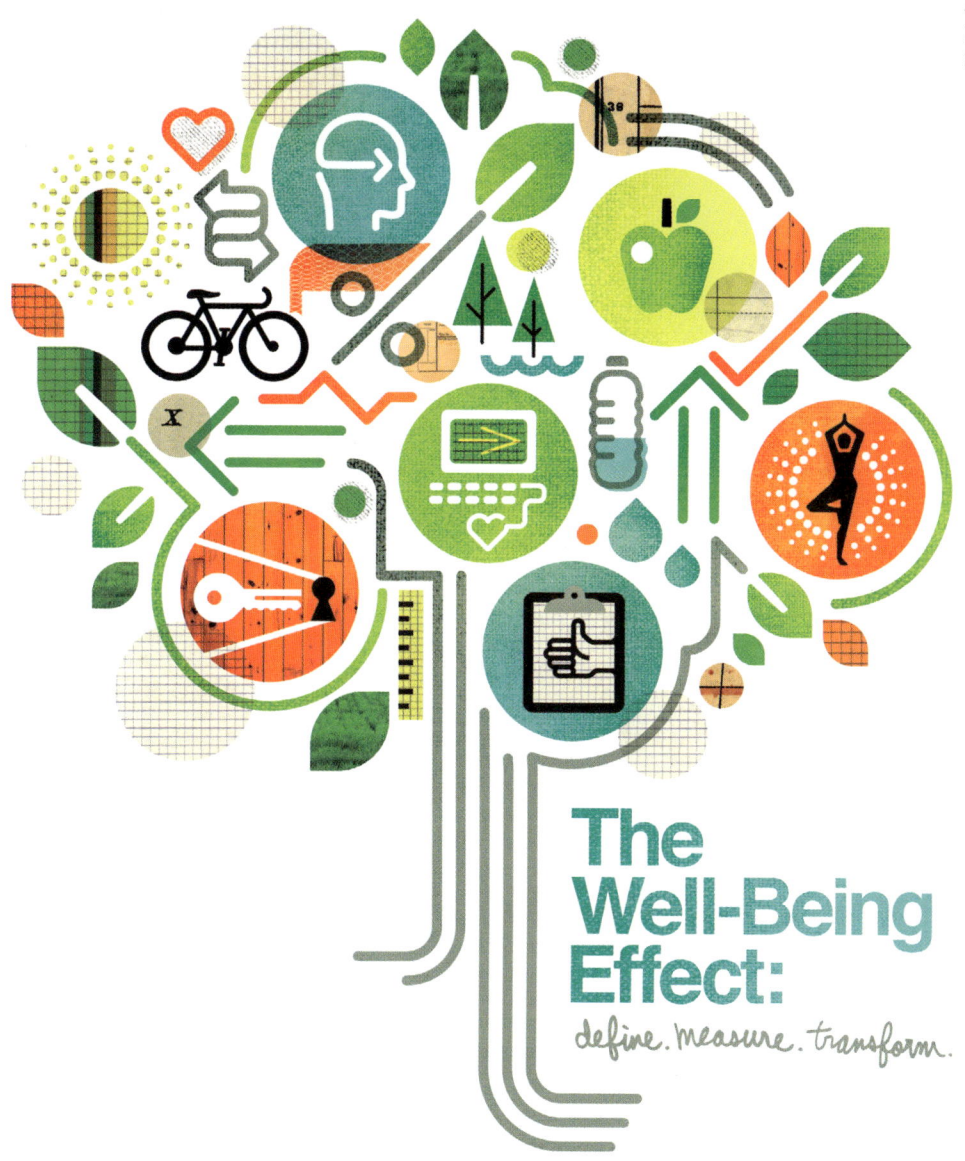

The Well-Being Effect:
define. measure. transform.

Monday	Tuesday	Wednesday	Thursday	Friday	Saturday	Sunday
10	11	12	13	14	15	16

JUNE

Matthew Korbel-Bowers

Monday	Tuesday	Wednesday	Thursday	Friday	Saturday	Sunday
17	18	19	20	21	22	23

JUNE

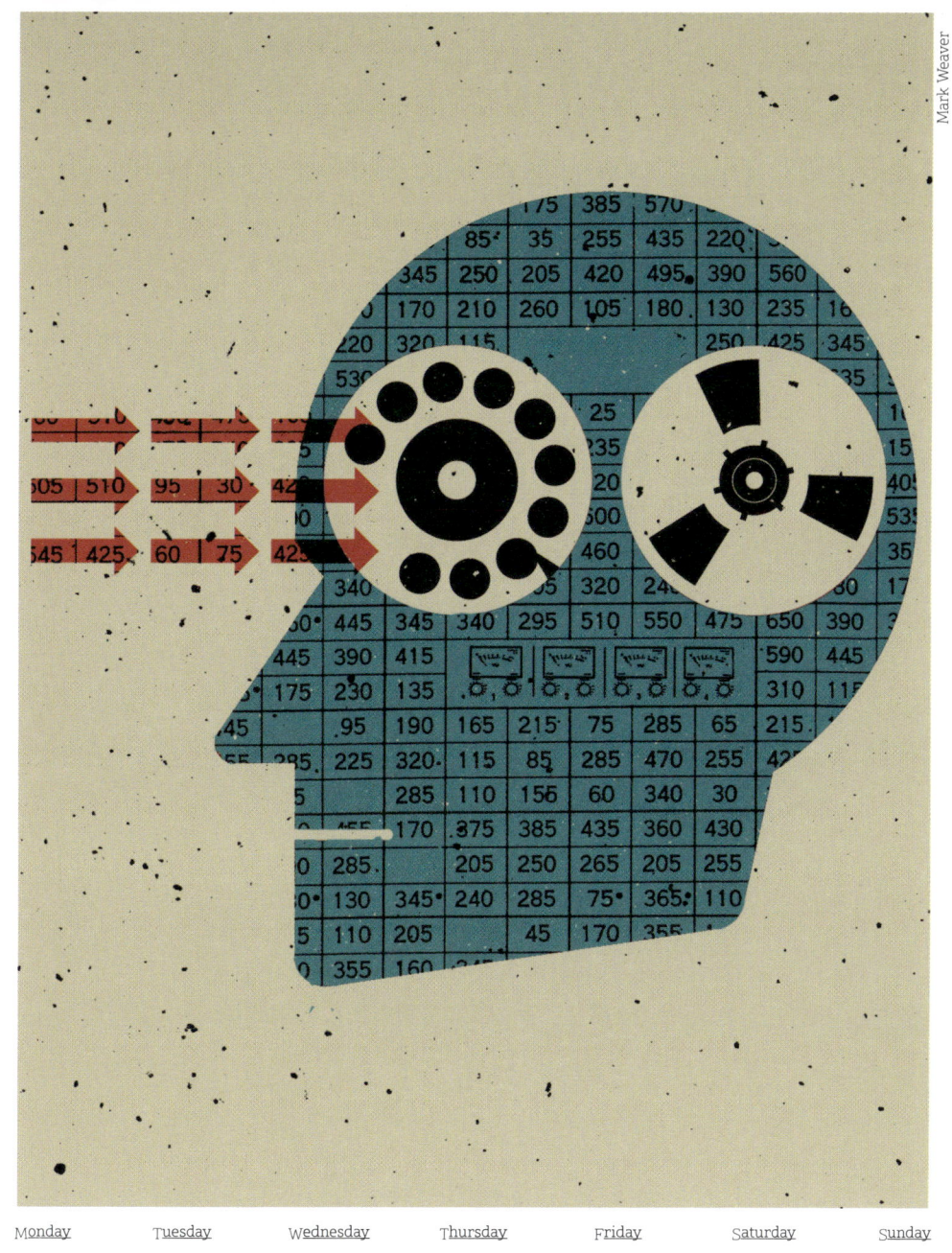

Monday	Tuesday	Wednesday	Thursday	Friday	Saturday	Sunday
24	25	26	27	28	29	30

JUNE

PARTICLE ACCELERATION

$E = mc^2$: all begins with Einstein's famous equation. It simply states that mass and energy are the same thing, and can thus be turned into one another. How awesome is that?

All rights reserved. Artwork © 2013
Mark Brooks Graphic Design,
Santamonica Records.

www.santamonica.com

SantaMonica
LegitimateWear

Mark Brooks

Monday	Tuesday	Wednesday	Thursday	Friday	Saturday	Sunday
01	02	03	04	05	06	07

JULY

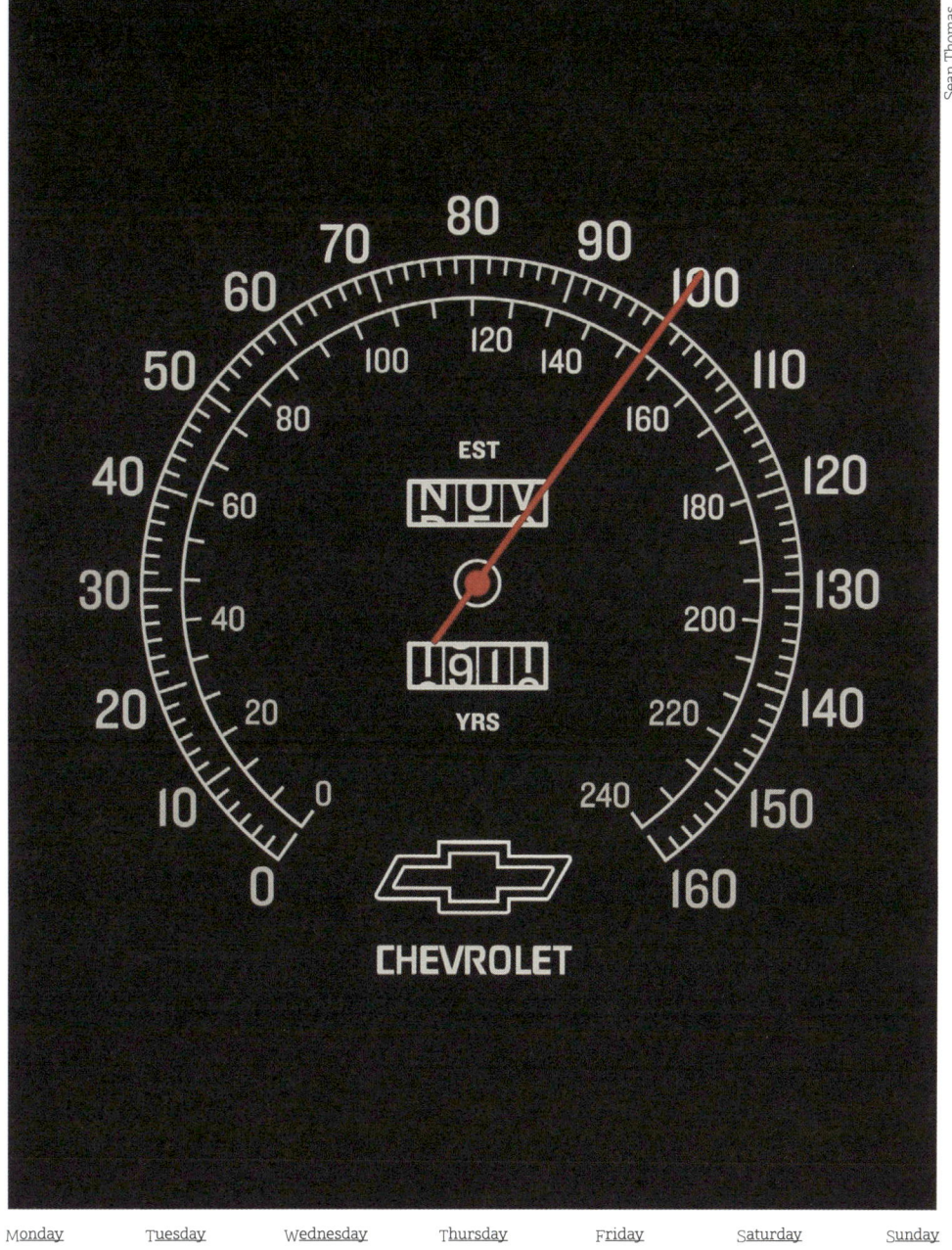

Monday	Tuesday	Wednesday	Thursday	Friday	Saturday	Sunday
08	09	10	11	12	13	14

JULY

Sean Thomas

Duane Dalton

Monday	Tuesday	Wednesday	Thursday	Friday	Saturday	Sunday
15	16	17	18	19	20	21

JULY

PRODUCED IN ASSOCIATION WITH LIVE NATION & THE LAKESIDE GROUP

The National

WITH SPECIAL GUEST OKKERVIL RIVER MARYMOOR PARK 9/11/10 AT 7PM

Invisible Creature, Inc.

Monday	Tuesday	Wednesday	Thursday	Friday	Saturday	Sunday
22	23	24	25	26	27	28

JULY

REPUBLICA DE LA BOCA

BsAs

Monday	Tuesday	Wednesday	Thursday	Friday	Saturday	Sunday
29	30	31	01	02	03	04

AUGUST

NEW YORK

★ ★ ★ ★ ★

Cristiana Couceiro

**TRAVELS
WITH MY AUNT**

Monday	Tuesday	Wednesday	Thursday	Friday	Saturday	Sunday
05	06	07	08	09	10	11

AUGUST

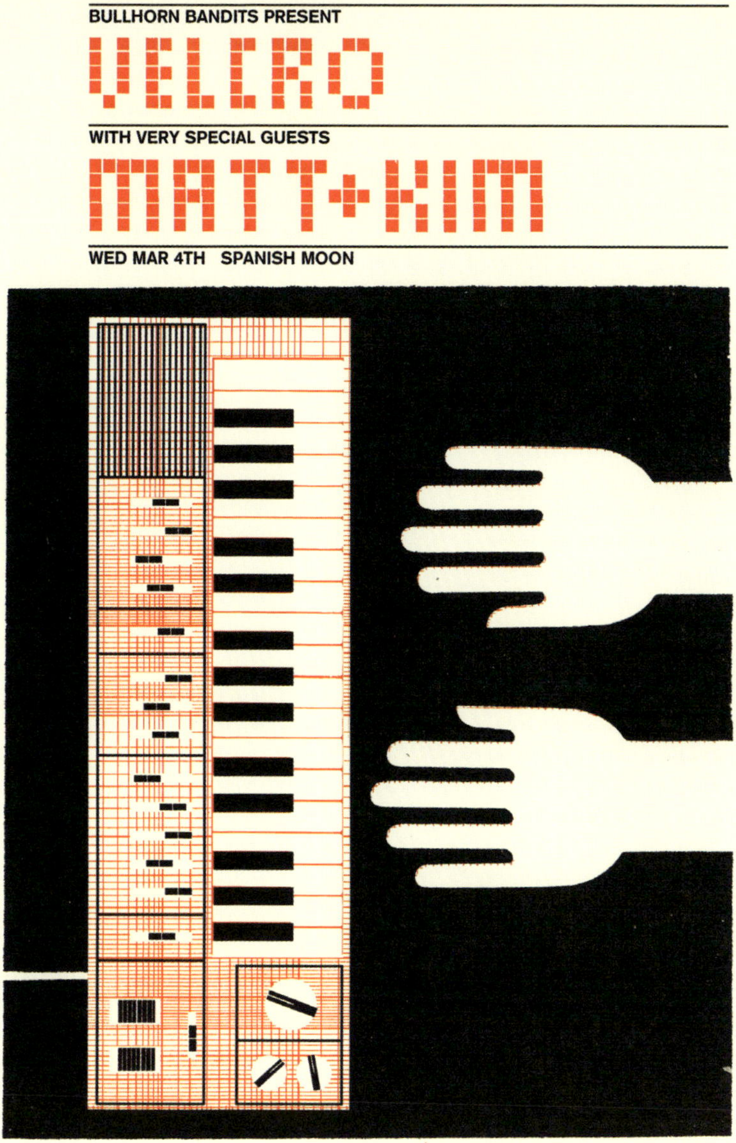

Scott Campbell

Monday	Tuesday	Wednesday	Thursday	Friday	Saturday	Sunday
12	13	14	15	16	17	18

AUGUST

Timba Smits

Monday	Tuesday	Wednesday	Thursday	Friday	Saturday	Sunday
19	20	21	22	23	24	25

AUGUST

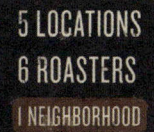

Jason Permenter

Tenderloin
COFFEE CRAWL
SAN FRANCISCO, CALIFORNIA

little bird | CON TRA BAN | farm : table | HOOKER'S sweet treats

SATURDAY 2-5 PM **FEB 5**[TH] **2011** **5 LOCATIONS / 6 ROASTERS / 1 NEIGHBORHOOD**

HOSTED BY FARM:TABLE   VISIT HTTP://FARMTABLESF.COM/COFFEECRAWL

Monday	Tuesday	Wednesday	Thursday	Friday	Saturday	Sunday
26	27	28	29	30	01	02

SEPTEMBER

"I HAVE A DREAM"

**MARTIN LUTHER KING
AUGUST 1963**

Telegramme Studio

Monday	Tuesday	Wednesday	Thursday	Friday	Saturday	Sunday
03	04	05	06	07	08	09

SEPTEMBER

Concepción Studios

Monday	Tuesday	Wednesday	Thursday	Friday	Saturday	Sunday
10	11	12	13	14	15	16

SEPTEMBER

Silence TV

**SILENCE TELEVISION
ILLUSTRATIONS & PRINTS**

Monday	Tuesday	Wednesday	Thursday	Friday	Saturday	Sunday
17	18	19	20	21	22	23

SEPTEMBER

THE MOUNTAIN GOATS

JUNE 16, 2010 / URBAN LOUNGE / SALT LAKE CITY, UT

with **THE BEETS**

Jason Munn

Monday	Tuesday	Wednesday	Thursday	Friday	Saturday	Sunday
24	25	26	27	28	29	30

SEPTEMBER

Monday	Tuesday	Wednesday	Thursday	Friday	Saturday	Sunday
31	01	02	03	04	05	06

OCTOBER

the colored dots
francine lombardo

the infamous press

Morten Iveland

Monday	Tuesday	Wednesday	Thursday	Friday	Saturday	Sunday
07	08	09	10	11	12	13

OCTOBER

Timba Smits

Monday	Tuesday	Wednesday	Thursday	Friday	Saturday	Sunday
14	15	16	17	18	19	20

OCTOBER

Doublenaut

AGENCY DOMINION 2010

Monday	Tuesday	Wednesday	Thursday	Friday	Saturday	Sunday
21	22	23	24	25	26	27

OCTOBER

Brandon Schaefer

TWO THOUSAND AND ONE
A SPACE ODYSSEY

A STANLEY KUBRICK FILM
STARRING KIER DULLEA · GARY LOCKWOOD
SCREENPLAY BY STANLEY KUBRICK & ARTHUR C. CLARKE · FILMED IN SUPER PANAVISION & METROCOLOR

Monday	Tuesday	Wednesday	Thursday	Friday	Saturday	Sunday
28	29	30	31	01	02	03

NOVEMBER

Mike Krol

Monday	Tuesday	Wednesday	Thursday	Friday	Saturday	Sunday
04	05	06	07	08	09	10

NOVEMBER

SAN TELMO
BUENOS AIRES

Monday	Tuesday	Wednesday	Thursday	Friday	Saturday	Sunday
11	12	13	14	15	16	17

NOVEMBER

Lawerta

WAR OF THE WORLDS — H.G. WELLS

Brandon Schaefer

Monday	Tuesday	Wednesday	Thursday	Friday	Saturday	Sunday
18	19	20	21	22	23	24

NOVEMBER

Monday	Tuesday	Wednesday	Thursday	Friday	Saturday	Sunday
25	26	27	28	29	30	01

DECEMBER

SPECIALS of the MONTH

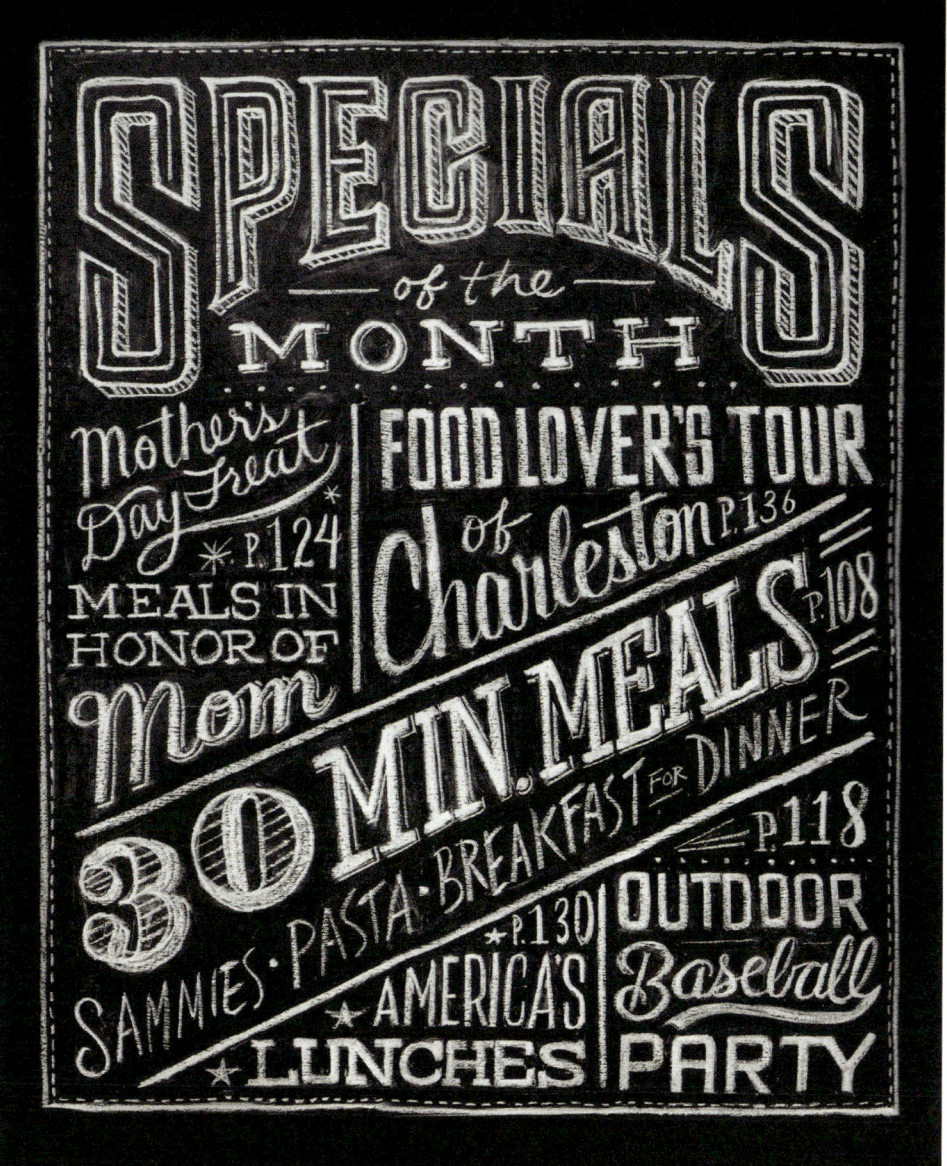

- Mother's Day Treat *P.124* — Meals in Honor of Mom
- Food Lover's Tour of Charleston *P.136*
- 30 Min. Meals *P.108* — Sammies · Pasta · Breakfast for Dinner
- America's Lunches *P.130*
- Outdoor Baseball Party *P.118*

Dana Tanamachi

Monday	Tuesday	Wednesday	Thursday	Friday	Saturday	Sunday
02	03	04	05	06	07	08

DECEMBER

Concepción Studios

DEFTONES
DIAMOND EYES
TOUR / 10

Monday	Tuesday	Wednesday	Thursday	Friday	Saturday	Sunday
09	10	11	12	13	14	15

DECEMBER

Marius Roosendaal

Monday	Tuesday	Wednesday	Thursday	Friday	Saturday	Sunday
16	17	18	19	20	21	22

DECEMBER

Darling Clementine

Monday	Tuesday	Wednesday	Thursday	Friday	Saturday	Sunday
23	24	25	26	27	28	29

DECEMBER

Brandan Deason

CONSUMED with CHRIST

FALLS CREEK OKLAHOMA

Camp June 2011

Monday	Tuesday	Wednesday	Thursday	Friday	Saturday	Sunday
30	31	01	02	03	04	05

DECEMBER

Cover illustration: Mark Weaver, mrkwvr.com
Typefaces: Treza by Benjamin Gomez, Nautinger by Moritz Esser
Foundry: www.gestaltenfonts.com

Andaur Studio	swork.andaurstudios.cl
Astronaut Design	www.astronautdesign.com
Brandan Deason	cargocollective.com/brandandeason
Brandon Schaefer	www.seekandspeak.com
Concepción Studios	www.concepcionstudios.com
Cristiana Couceiro	www.cristianacouceiro.com
Dana Tanamachi	www.danatanamachi.com
Darling Clementine	www.darlingclementine.no
Doublenaut	www.doublenaut.com
Duane Dalton	cargocollective.com/duanedalton
Heath Killen	heathkillen.com
Invisible Creature, Inc.	www.invisiblecreature.com
Jason Munn	www.jasonmunn.com
Jason Permenter	work.jasonpermenter.com
Jonathan Mutch	www.jonmutch.com
Julian Montague	www.montagueprojects.com
Kelli Anderson	kellianderson.com
La Boca	www.laboca.co.uk
Lawerta	www.lawerta.com
Marius Roosendaal	mariusroosendaal.com
Mark Brooks	www.markbrooksgraphikdesign.com
Mark Weaver	mrkwvr.com
Matt Lehman	mattlehmanstudio.com
Matthew Korbel-Bowers	korbelbowers.com
Mike Krol	mikekrol.com
Morten Iveland	cargocollective.com/iveland
Riley Cran	www.rileycran.com
Scott Campbell	scttcmpbll.com
Sean Thomas	whatarogue.com
Silence TV	www.silencetv.com
Telegramme Studio	www.telegramme.co.uk
Timba Smits	www.timbasmits.com

Stargazer Calendar 2013

Published by Gestalten · ISBN 978-3-89955-425-0 · Printed in China
© Die Gestalten Verlag GmbH & Co. KG, Berlin 2012

All rights reserved. No part of this publication may be reproduced or transmitted in any form or by any means, electronic or mechanical, including photocopy or any storage and retrieval system, without permission in writing from the publisher.

For more information, please visit www.gestalten.com.
Respect copyrights, encourage creativity!

IMPRINT